DREAM, PLAN, GROW

The Ultimate Business Guide for Solopreneurs

A five-step workbook + planner for building
and growing your business

By Ariana Nicole

ariananicoledesigns.com

GREETINGS AND
WELCOME

Hello Fellow 'Preneur!

I'm so excited you're ready to push your business to the next level!

This workbook is designed to help solopreneurs, (like yourself) transform passion into profit. Each step has a series of questions and activities to help you build a strong, profitable foundation for your business and strategize your moneymaking ideas. Having a plan along with custom brand and web design is just what your business needs to grow and succeed. Inside you will find these five steps:

☐ STEP 1 - CREATE A PLAN pages 7-13

☐ STEP 2 - RESEARCH YOUR AUDIENCE pages 17-21

☐ STEP 3 - IMPLEMENT YOUR STRATEGY pages 25-27

☐ STEP 4 - MANAGE YOUR INCOME pages 31-35

☐ STEP 5 - DREAM BIG! pages 39-41

So grab a pen, make some coffee, and get comfortable.
It's time to start building the business of your dreams!

Your brand and web designer,

Ariana Nicole

CREATE A PLAN

Use the Solopreneur's Business Plan to
create a blueprint for your business

"It's not the plan that's important, it's the planning."

- Dr. Gramme Edwards

INTRODUCTION

Every great business starts with a plan. Understanding what you want to achieve and what you need to make it happen is key to building and growing your business. Use this business plan to clarify your thoughts and create measurable goals to achieve them.

IN THIS SECTION YOU WILL:

✓ Define your business

✓ Create short- and long-term goals

✓ Project business costs

✓ Recognize your competitors

✓ Set the tone for your brand

HELPFUL SIDENOTES

Pencil in answers you're unsure about, so you can easily edit later.

Share your plans and ideas with other solopreneurs for feedback.

Review and revise your business plan around every 5-6 months.

WORDS TO KNOW

Business Plan: a written document that describes your business in detail

Mission Statement: a declaration that explains the purpose for your business

Passive Income: a steady stream of income that requires little-to-no effort to maintain

Niche Competitor: a business that targets an identical audience and/or offers similar products or services

BUSINESS PLAN

A good business plan is the key to good business. Similar to a blueprint, it lays out all the elements you'll need to really build your business. Complete the following sections to organize your thoughts and ideas.

Talk About What You Do

Mission Statement

What is the purpose of your business? What makes your business stand out from other solopreneurs in your field? *If you get stuck, feel free to answer the other sections first and return to this one later.*

_____

_____

_____

_____

_____

_____

_____

Background Info

What is your business niche? Are you a blogger, freelancer, shop owner, event planner, etc.? Do you offer products, services or both? Why are you qualified to provide these products and/or services?

_____

_____

_____

_____

_____

_____

_____

_____

Do you intend to be a solopreneur forever? Are you interested in seeking a partnership or hiring employees in the future? What is your role in your business?

_____

_____

_____

_____

_____

_____

_____

BUSINESS PLAN

Think About The Future

What dreams do you have for your business? How do you define success?

_____
_____
_____
_____
_____
_____
_____
_____
_____

Describe what you want your business to look like in the next:

Month:

-
-
-

6 Months:

-
-
-

Year

-
-
-

3 Years:

-
-
-

The Solopreneur's
BUSINESS PLAN

Analyze The Costs

How much money will you need for your business? For products, consider production and shipping costs and for services, think about the resources you will need to build your skills (like a training course or certification program). Also, consider the costs of your work environment - will you work from home or rent a coworking space?

_____

_____

_____

_____

_____

_____

_____

_____

Budget Projections

How much money do you expect your business to make? Compare them to your predicted expenses above.

	Predicted Expenses	Expected Profits
At Start-Up		
Three Months		
Six Months		
1 Year		
2 Years		

BUSINESS PLAN

Other Logistics

How will your customers pay you? Will you accept deposits or require the amount in full? Will you need to use an online service to charge your customers? Does this service require a purchase? Do they charge any type of fees?

Do you plan to ship or deliver your goods? Are your services packaged together or available a la carte? How will you explain this process to your customers?

Passive Income

Outside income is especially beneficial for solopreneurs because it can help balance out your cash flow during a slow season. Circle any of the ideas below you can use to generate passive income for your business.

MONETIZE A BLOG	PROVIDE REFERRALS	SELL AN ONLINE COURSE
INVEST IN A START-UP	START A YOUTUBE CHANNEL	CREATE AN APP
PROMOTE AFFILIATE PRODUCTS	MAKE DIGITAL GOODS	OFFER MEMBERSHIP SUBSCRIPTIONS
SELL STOCK PHOTOS	BUILD AN EMAIL FUNNEL	EXPLORE NETWORK MARKETING

Use the blank spaces above to come up with a few of your own!

The Solopreneur's
BUSINESS PLAN

Know Your Competitors

Competitive Analysis

Which businesses do you consider your competition? What are their strengths? What are their weaknesses?

_____
_____
_____
_____
_____

Now what are the strengths of *your* business? What are *your* weaknesses?

_____
_____
_____
_____
_____

What type of risks does your business face when competing with others?

_____
_____
_____
_____

Consider Your Customer

How can you encourage customers to stay loyal to your business?

_____
_____
_____
_____
_____

What are the top three things customers can expect to gain when working with you?

-
-
-

NOTES

Creative juices still flowing? Jot down quick thoughts and ideas here!

RESEARCH YOUR AUDIENCE

Create a customer persona for your business with the following worksheet

"There is only one winning strategy. It is carefully define the target market and direct a superior offering to that target market."

- Lewis Howes

INTRODUCTION

It helps to know who will purchase your goods and services. Trying to appeal to everyone can result in wasted time and energy. In order to consider your customers' needs, goals and limitations, you have to know who and where they are.

IN THIS SECTION YOU WILL:

✓ Discover your ideal customer

✓ Identify your customers' needs

✓ Analyze your creative competitors

✓ Find your target audience

✓ Assess your current audience

HELPFUL SIDENOTES

Try thinking of someone you know (or want to work with) when creating in your customer persona.

Embrace the details! Be as specific as possible when describing your ideal customer.

Attend local meet-ups and events that your target audience is drawn toward.

WORDS TO KNOW

Ideal Customer: someone who respects what you offer and understands your value

Demographics: informational characteristics about your ideal customer (gender, age, etc.)

Target Audience: the intended group and focus for your business

Pain point: a specific customer need

Niche: the specialized market or industry for your business

Targeting Your Audience
WORKSHEET

Knowing your target audience will give you a better idea of how to market your business.
Complete the following sections to discover your ideal customer!

Ideal Customer Profile

Gender?

Age?

Location?

Education?

Income Level?

Industry?

Interests?

Passions?

List 4 words to describe your ideal customer's personality:

_____

_____

_____

_____

What does your customer do for a living?

_____
_____
_____
_____

What are some of your customer's pain points? What do they need?

_____
_____
_____

Niche and Competitors

What does your business do to resolve these needs?

_____
_____
_____
_____

What other solopreneurs have the ability to fulfill the same needs?

_____
_____
_____
_____

Discovering Your
TARGET AUDIENCE

Would you buy from your closest competitor? Why or why not?

_____

_____

_____

How can you implement (or avoid implementing) the above in your own business?

_____

_____

_____

What will customers say when referring your business to someone else?

_____

_____

List three questions someone could have about your business, products or services:

-
-
-

Social Media

Think about the type of social media networks your customer uses. Determine how often they use each network and research the best times for you to post. Then brainstorm the type of content you can post to attract and target your ideal audience.

	Level	Post Times	Content Ideas
Pinterest			
Twitter			
Google+			
Facebook			
Instagram			
YouTube			

Frequency Levels: **HEAVILY** - Hourly | **OFTEN** - Daily | **SOMETIMES** - Weekly | **RARELY** - Monthly | **NEVER** - Not at all

Discovering Your
TARGET AUDIENCE

Evaluate Your Current Audience

Describe the type of customers you work with now. How do they compare to your ideal customer profile?

_____
_____
_____
_____
_____
_____

How do the majority of your customers find you? Word-of-mouth? Online? Social media? Traditional advertising? Evaluate how well this method(s) works to reach your current audience and how well it will work for your ideal one.

_____
_____
_____
_____
_____

How many of your customers are new? How many are returning? What can you do to increase both?

_____
_____
_____
_____

What do you think motivates your customers to buy from you?

_____
_____
_____

Now find out why they really do! Brainstorm 5 or 6 questions you can ask your customers in a survey to get feedback about your products and services:

1. _____ ?

2. _____ ?

3. _____ ?

4. _____ ?

5. _____ ?

6. _____ ?

DOODLE

Have some fun visualizing your audience! Imagine your ideal customer, then sketch a picture below. Try incoporating elements that tell more about who they are (i.e. their hobbies, where they live, etc.).

IMPLEMENT
YOUR STRATEGY

Use the Strategic Marketing Checklist to
brainstorm ways you can market your business

❝

"Without a strategy, marketing is just stuff.
The world has enough stuff. Be intentional."

– Kurt Uhlir

INTRODUCTION

A marketing strategy is a comprehensive plan used to promote your brand and target a specific audience. Solopreneurs thrive with good and consistent marketing! A strong strategic plan can help you gain publicity, increase sales and distinguish your business from other niche competitors.

IN THIS SECTION YOU WILL:

✓ Learn new marketing strategies

✓ Prioritize your marketing ideas

✓ Brainstorm your own strategies

✓ Implement your marketing plan

HELPFUL SIDENOTES

A strong online presence is truly the backbone to marketing your business. Tweet @Ariana_Nicole__ using #DreamPlanGrow for special website pricing!

The lower a strategy is on the checklist, the more effort it will take to execute. Be logical when creating your plan.

WORDS TO KNOW

Marketing Plan: a series of steps or strategies used to reach a target audience

SEO Keywords: selected words or phrases used to index a webpage for higher search engine rankings

Inbound Marketing: content created primarily to attract an audience (i.e. blogs, podcasts, videos, etc.)

Analytics: a collection of data used to measure and analyze a strategy's progres

The Strategic
MARKETING CHECKLIST

Finding effective ways to market your business is key to its success. Strategic marketing helps build publicity and can set you apart from competitors. Explore the marketing strategies you can use to reach your target audience in the checklist below, then fill in a few strategies of your own. Use the bar on the right to estimate the level of effort it will take you to implement each one.

SOCIAL MEDIA

FACEBOOK
- ☐ Create a page
- ☐ Start a group
- ☐ Go LIVE!

TWITTER
- ☐ Take a poll
- ☐ @ new followers
- ☐ Join a chat

INSTAGRAM
- ☐ Run a contest
- ☐ Use ☺☺☺'s
- ☐ Add a #hashtag

PINTEREST
- ☐ Set up rich pins
- ☐ Join group boards
- ☐ Use large graphics

LOW

INBOUND
- ☐ Launch a blog
- ☐ Try out podcasting
- ☐ Record "How-To" videos
- ☐ _____

EMAIL
- ☐ Offer special pricing
- ☐ Take a survey
- ☐ Send an announcement or update
- ☐ _____

MEDIUM

PAID
- ☐ Utilize the **Creative Circle***
- ☐ Try Google AdWords
- ☐ Use traditional advertising
- ☐ _____

SEO
- ☐ Shrink your images for faster speed
- ☐ Add outbound links to your posts
- ☐ Research and adopt new keywords
- ☐ _____

HIGH

EVENTS
- ☐ Throw a launch party!
- ☐ Host a meet-up for your niche
- ☐ Attend a class or conference
- ☐ _____

COMMUNITY
- ☐ Do pro bono work
- ☐ Team up with a fellow creative
- ☐ Ship free goodies to new customers!
- ☐ _____

Access or join the Creative Circle by visiting ArianaNicoleDesigns.com/Creative-Circle

NOTES

Creative juices still flowing? Jot down quick thoughts and ideas here!

MANAGE YOUR INCOME

Use the Financial Organizer
to predict and calculate your cash flow

"Money is only a tool. It will take you wherever you wish, but it will not replace you as the driver."

- Ayn Rand

INTRODUCTION

Every solopreneur faces the risk of running out of money. It's important to have a financial plan to monitor and predict cash flow and business expenses. Having a thorough understanding of these numbers will help you grow a steady and profitable income for your business.

IN THIS SECTION YOU WILL:

✓ Brainstorm revenue streams

✓ Analyze your expenses

✓ Set your prices

✓ Estimate your monthly income

WORDS TO KNOW

Multiple Revenue Streams: Additional income sources outside of your main products and services

Cash Flow: The total amount of money moving in and out of your business

Business Account: An independent account used to track and monitor business finances

Fixed Expenses: Costs that remain the same over a period of time

HELPFUL SIDENOTES

Grab a pencil, eraser and a calculator (or your cell phone) to do the math.

Don't be afraid to charge what you're worth, but keep your target market in mind.

Try not to skip around - many of your answers will be based off the ones in the section before it.

The Solopreneur's
FINANCIAL ORGANIZER

Passion is great, but money is a must to keep your business running! Complete the sections below to calculate your monthly expenses and predict your total income.

Diversify Your Income

It's never wise to put all your eggs in one basket, especially when it comes to your income. Did you know the average millionaire has *seven different* sources of revenue? Prepare your business for success by listing out seven (or more!) ways you can generate income.

1. _____
2. _____
3. _____
4. _____

5. _____
6. _____
7. _____
8. _____

^^^ THIS ONE GETS BONUS POINTS! ^^^

As a solopreneur it might be difficult implementing these all at once. Circle the revenue streams you want to focus on now and take note of things you want to do in the future.

Predicted Expenses

Now write down all your monthly expenses for both your business **and** your personal life. Having a numerical understanding of both these costs can help you better determine prices for your products and services.

	EXPENSE LIST	🔒	PREDICTION	ACTUAL	DIFFERENCE
PERSONAL	Rent	✓	$850	$822	+$28
BUSINESS					

MONTH: _____

🔒 - Fixed Expense   TOTALS:

FINANCIAL ORGANIZER

Pricing

Now think about what you want to charge your customers for your products and/or services. List everything you want to offer and consider what you'll need to invest to make it happen. "Costs" refers to the money spent to make and sell your products and "Time" obviously addresses the amount of minutes, hours, days, etc it takes you to provide your services.

Products	Costs	Price	Services	Time	Price

Ultimately, you want your prices to be profitable and truly reflect the value of what you do.
Be sure to consider the following when determining your prices:

☐ **TAXES**
factor them in now to avoid
headaches from the IRS later

☐ **PAYMENT PROCESS**
how consumers pay can affect
the timing of your income

☐ **PRODUCTION & DELIVERY COSTS**
the amount you earn should outweigh
the amount you spend

☐ **SKILL LEVEL**
your prices should reflect
your experience

☐ **CONSUMER VALUE**
what consumers gain from
your product/service

☐ **PERSONAL LEAVE**
you can't work all the time
and you shouldn't have to

FINANCIAL ORGANIZER

Income Projections

Reference the previous page to complete the chart below. Under "Quantity," estimate the number of products and services you will sell and multiply that number by your price to predict your earnings for the month. Then use this sheet to track your actual earnings and calculate your income total.

MONTH: _____

Product/Service	PREDICTION		ACTUAL	
	Quantity	Earnings	Quantity	Earnings
	___ x ___ =	$	___ x ___ =	$
	___ x ___ =	$	___ x ___ =	$
	___ x ___ =	$	___ x ___ =	$
	___ x ___ =	$	___ x ___ =	$
	___ x ___ =	$	___ x ___ =	$
	___ x ___ =	$	___ x ___ =	$
	___ x ___ =	$	___ x ___ =	$
	___ x ___ =	$	___ x ___ =	$
	___ x ___ =	$	___ x ___ =	$
	___ x ___ =	$	___ x ___ =	$
	___ x ___ =	$	___ x ___ =	$
	___ x ___ =	$	___ x ___ =	$
	___ x ___ =	$	___ x ___ =	$
	___ x ___ =	$	___ x ___ =	$
	___ x ___ =	$	___ x ___ =	$
	___ x ___ =	$	___ x ___ =	$
		TOTAL:		TOTAL:

Now it's time to do the math! Transfer your answers from page 16 to calculate your predicted and actual income.

WRITE YOUR **EARNINGS** HERE: [____] [____]

—

WRITE YOUR **EXPENSES** HERE: [____] [____]

SUBTRACT THE TWO ABOVE TO GET YOUR **TOTAL PROFIT**: [____] [____]

The gray box reveals what you expect to make for the month. While the purple one shows how much you're actually making. If these numbers aren't where you want them to be, don't get discouraged! Getting brand and web design with me will add value to your business and ultimately help increase both of these totals.

A|N

NOTES

Mental math not your thing? Use the space below to write out your calculations.

DREAM BIG!

Achieve success for your business with
the Goal Planning Worksheet

"It's quite fun to do the impossible."

- Walt Disney

INTRODUCTION

Writing specific goals for your business is the first step to making them happen. Goals create purpose and help narrow your focus to what's most important for achieving them. Seeing your goals written down on paper is a great source of motivation and helps build your commitment to getting them done.

IN THIS SECTION YOU WILL:

✓ Visualize your dreams

✓ Write down your business goals

✓ Plan the steps to reach your goals

HELPFUL SIDENOTES

Write ALL your goals and ideas down, even the ones that may sound far-fetched.

The more specific you are with your goals, the easier it will be to create action steps.

Reference your calendar throughout the year and mark off your goals as you complete them.

WORDS TO KNOW

Measurable Goals: Goals with a numerical value used to measure your degree of success (i.e. a date, amount, percentage, etc.)

Attainable Goals: Goals that push the limits, but are still possible to achieve

Passion: A source of motivation for accomplishing your business goals

Creative Visionary: An entrepreneur with big dreams for their business and high hopes for the future

The Goal Planning
WORKSHEET

As a solopreneur, the sky is your limit! It's important to dream big for your business and set goals for yourself. Use this sheet to record your goals, then plan out the steps to make them happen!

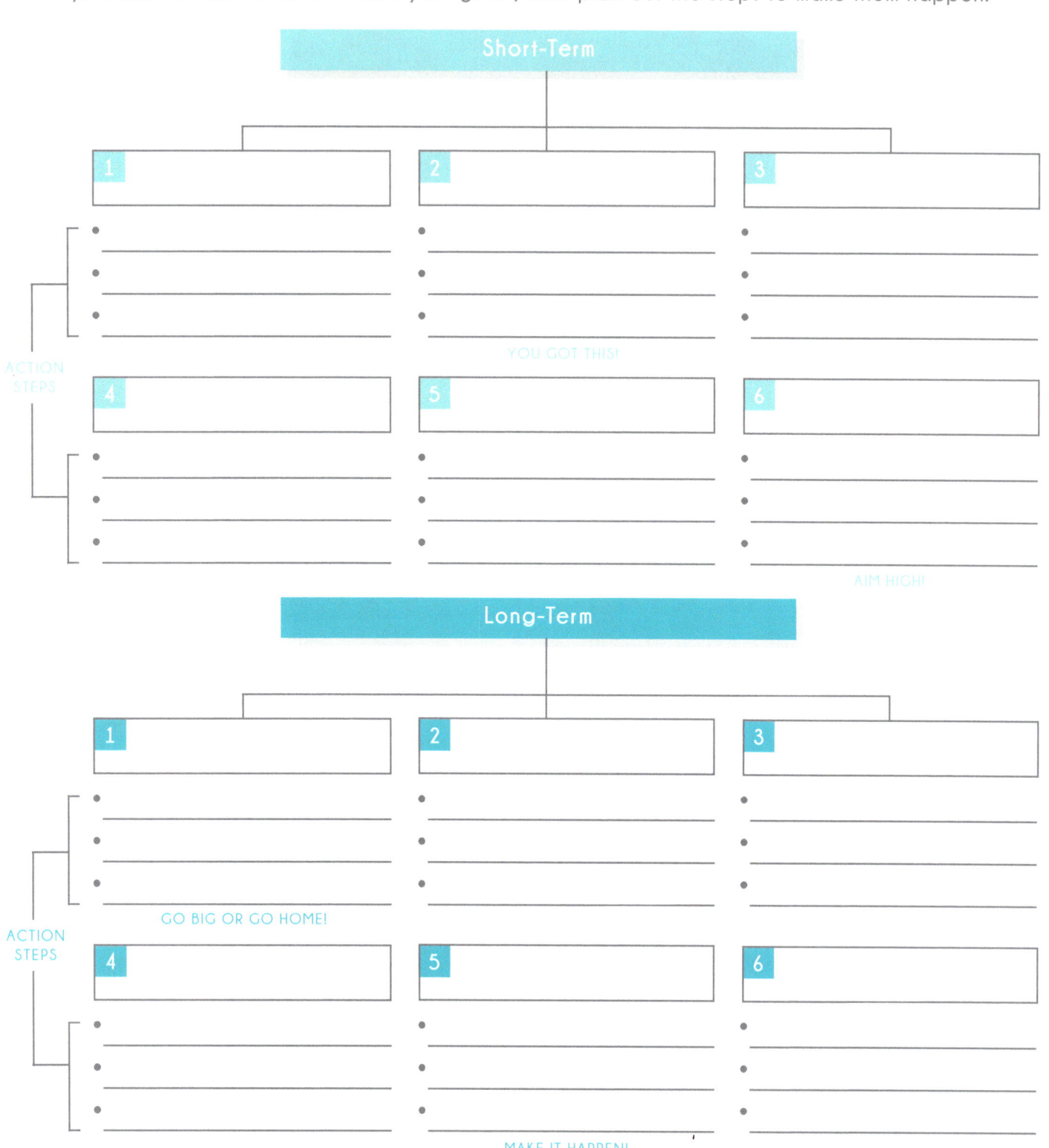

Short-Term

| 1 | 2 | 3 |

ACTION STEPS

YOU GOT THIS!

| 4 | 5 | 6 |

AIM HIGH!

Long-Term

| 1 | 2 | 3 |

ACTION STEPS

GO BIG OR GO HOME!

| 4 | 5 | 6 |

MAKE IT HAPPEN!

Now get ready to put these steps into action! Instagram a photo of your goals worksheet with the hastag #DreamPlanGrow to get a FREE calendar you can use to plan out your action steps.

NOTES

Creative juices still flowing? Jot down quick thoughts and ideas here!

#DreamPlanGrow

Congratulations! You've successfully planned and organized your business. Now you're ready to take the next step: creating your brand identity. Solopreneurs need consistent branding and a compelling web presence to truly be successful in today's digital world. Potential consumers will use their experience with your brand and website to decide whether (or not) they'll be your next loyal customer, reader, viewer, client, etc.

It takes more than "just a logo" to build a strong, memorable brand. You'll need the complete creative package and my design services are tailored to be a "one-stop shop" for all your business needs. My design packages include helpful business resources, in addition to professional brand and web design. I will build your brand beyond *"just a logo"* and connect you with other solopreneurs who are here to help you grow your business into the one of your dreams.

READY TO GET STARTED?
Visit www.ariananicoledesigns.com/work-with-me

www.ingramcontent.com/pod-product-compliance
Lightning Source LLC
Chambersburg PA
CBHW050904180526
45159CB00007B/2781